COMPARED WITH MEN, women in 21st-century America live five years longer; face an unemployment rate that is significantly lower; are awarded a substantially larger share of high school diplomas, BAs, and MAs; and face lower rates of incarceration, alcoholism, and drug abuse. In other words, contrary to what feminist lobbyists would have Congress believe, girls and women are doing well.

With these data before us, reasonable individuals should be holding conferences on how to help men get more education and employment opportunities. Policymakers should require that government contractors hire men to bring down their 10 percent unemployment rate. Health reform bills should feature Offices of Men's Health to help men live to the same age as women.

Unfortunately, the reverse is occurring. Both Congress and President Obama continue to advocate policies that favor women over men. The new financial regulation bill has mandated the creation of 29 offices to help the advancement of women. The recently passed health reform law has set up multiple offices of women's health. President Obama wants to extend quotas now in place for women in university sports to science and math.

Much of this is motivated by congressional defensiveness in the face of fierce feminist lobbying that is largely unopposed. Once, feminists advocated equality of opportunity. Now that this has largely been achieved, they clamor for equal outcomes – a result that Congress prudently should not try to legislate. Equal outcomes is a pernicious goal for government policy, one that smacks of central planning and heavy official intrusion into private decision making, such as what to study and what vocation to pursue.

Women as a group spontaneously make choices that are different from men's, and there is nothing wrong with that. Of course, if professional feminists were to acknowledge the validity of these choices, they would put themselves out of business – and might have to make some other career choices of their own.

Congress also responds to data that show

differences in average wages between men and women. There is less to these differences than meets the eye. The gap almost disappears when the analysis accounts for gender differences in education, on-the-job experience, and the presence of children in the worker's household.

By rightly lobbying for equality of opportunity, feminists in the 1960s were sending the message that women can take care of themselves in the economy and in society. Helen Reddy's song "I Am Woman," top of the charts in 1972, contained the lyrics "I am strong, I am invincible, I am woman." Helen Reddy's woman was not intimidated by going into law and medicine, and the idea that she

---

Once, feminists advocated equality of opportunity. Now that this has largely been achieved, they clamor for equal outcomes.

---

would need affirmative action and quotas to go into science or finance contradicts the basic message that women are as strong as men.

In contrast, the 21st-century feminist message is that women are weak and need protection through special preferences. Not only does this harm men by depriving them of opportunities, but it harms women by invalidating their hard-earned credentials. Not even a woman would choose a female brain surgeon for delicate surgery if she knew that the surgeon was a product of affirmative action. Instead, the patient would choose a man, because he might be better at his job. Giving preferences to a few women sows seeds of doubt that reflect on all.

The great irony is that women succeed in everyday America but are doomed to failure in the distorted lens of official Washington. A woman who chooses a part-time job with a flexible schedule in order to have time both for her family and her career thinks of herself as successful. But to feminists, she is a failure because she is on a lower earnings path than a man and has not selected the chief executive officer track.

The Wage Gap and the Paycheck Fairness Act

Every year, usually in April, Democratic members of Congress hold hearings on pay differences between men and women. In 2009, it was New York Rep. Carolyn Maloney, and in 2010, in was Iowa Sen. Tom Harkin. The occasion is Equal Pay Day – the day of the year, according to feminists, when all full-time women's wages, allegedly only 80 percent of all men's in 2009, "catch up" to what men have earned the year before. The story is that women have to work those extra months to achieve equality.

Maloney declared at the 2009 hearing, "[W]e have considerable work left to do before women earn equal pay for equal work." And, in 2010, Harkin wrote, "Nearly half a century after Congress enacted the Equal Pay Act, too many women in this country still do not get paid what men do for the exact same work. On average, a woman makes only 77 cents for every dollar that a man makes."

No matter that the latest figures show that comparing men and women who work 40 hours weekly yields a wage ratio of 86 percent, even before accounting for different education, jobs, or experience, which brings the wage ratio closer to 95 percent. Many studies, such as those by Professor June O'Neill of Baruch College and Professor Marianne Bertrand of the University of Chicago, show that when women work at the same jobs as men, with the same accumulated lifetime work experience, they earn essentially the same salary.

Marriage and children explain a large part of the wage gap, because many mothers like to spend time with their children and value flexible schedules. The Yale Law Women Web page, the site for female law students at Yale Law School, reads, "In the aftermath of the recent global financial crisis, YLW believes that the focus on family friendly firm

Not even a woman would choose a female brain surgeon for delicate surgery if she knew that the surgeon was a product of affirmative action.

policies and policies designed for the retention of women remains more important and pressing than ever."

In addition to a desire for flexibility within full-time work, the U.S. Department of Labor reports that 26 percent of women chose to work part time in 2009. (Another 9 percent of all female workers, who usually worked full time, reported that they worked part time for "economic or noneconomic reasons.")

Labor Department data show that in 2009, single women working full time earned about 95 percent of men's earnings, but married women earned 76 percent of what married men earned. Married women with children between the ages of 6 and 17 earned 70 percent of the salaries of men with children of the same age.

Of course, children are not the only reason that women, on average, have lower earnings than men. Some people are paid less than others because of the choices they make about their field of study, occupation, and time on the job.

When these differences are considered, a 2009 study by the economics consulting firm CONSAD Research Corporation, prepared for President George W. Bush's Labor Department, shows that women make around 94 percent of what men make. The remaining gap is due to unexplained variables, one of which might be discrimination.

In order to solve the purported wage gap, Congress is considering the Paycheck Fairness Act, a bill designed to raise women's wages that was introduced by Secretary of State Hillary Clinton when she was still a Democratic senator from New York. The bill has 42 Democratic cosponsors, and it would vastly expand the role of the government in employers' compensation decisions.

The Paycheck Fairness Act was one of the first bills that the House of Representatives passed in January 2009, and, as of this writing, has been stalled in the Senate. It would require the government to collect information on workers' pay, by race and sex, with the goal of equalizing wages of men and women and raising women's wages. (Fortunately for men, depressing their wages to achieve pay equity is not permitted under the proposed law.)

On July 20, 2010, President Obama issued a statement calling for passage of the Paycheck Fairness bill. He declared, "Yet, even in 2010, women make only 77 cents for every dollar that men earn. . . . So today, I thank the House for its work on this issue and encourage the Senate to pass the Paycheck Fairness Act, a common-sense bill that will help ensure that men and women who do equal work receive the equal pay that they and their families deserve."

The bill is misnamed because it responds to a false problem. There is far less pay discrimination against women than professional feminists allege. When the data are understood correctly – accounting for choice of vocation and on-the-job years – the putative pay gap largely disappears. The professional feminists try to conceal that, lest they be out of business.

With numerous anti-discrimination laws, such as Title VII of the Civil Rights Act, the Equal Pay Act, and the Lilly Ledbetter Fair Pay Act (signed into law by President Obama in January 2009), women do not need more remedies for discrimination. Courts have sufficient tools, and they use them. The pending bill would only burden employers with more regulations and paperwork, further discouraging hiring – of men and women.

The Paycheck Fairness Act, if enacted, would spawn a tidal wave of lawsuits and enmesh employers in endless litigation. The bill is a full-employment act for lawyers that would further burden already overburdened courts.

The bill would only allow employers to defend differences in pay between men and women on the grounds of education, training, and experience if these factors are also justi-fied on the grounds of "business necessity." Jane McFetridge, a witness at the March 2010 Senate Committee on Health, Education, Labor and Pensions hearing and a partner with Jackson Lewis LLP, a Chicago law firm, testified that this change could prohibit male supermarket managers with college degrees from being paid more than female cashiers – because the college degree for the male man-ager might not be consistent with "business necessity."

Another provision of the Paycheck Fair-ness bill would expand the number of estab-lishments subject to the law from one to all establishments of the same employer in a county. Now, employees who do substantially the same work in one location have to be paid equally. Including all locations would mean that cashiers in high-cost or unpleasant areas, where the employer has to pay more to attract workers, have to be paid the same as those in low-cost, more pleasant areas. Identifying "substantially the same work" is hard to do for disparate jobs in different locations. The intent is to raise wages of employees at the lower end, driving up employment costs and encouraging layoffs.

Class-action suits would be facilitated by the bill's opt-out clause. Now, if a worker wants to participate in a class-action suit against her employer, she has to affirmatively agree to take part, or opt in. Under the bill, she would automatically be included unless she opted out. This provision would increase the numbers in class-action suits and would be a boon to plaintiffs' lawyers.

Penalties that the courts could levy on employers would be heavier, too. Under the law now, employers found guilty of discrimination owe workers back pay. Under the pending bill, they would have to pay punitive damages, of which a quarter or a third typically goes to plaintiffs' lawyers.

The bill would require the Equal Employment Opportunity Commission to analyze pay data and promulgate regulations to collect more data, including information about the sex, race, and national origin of employees. The paperwork required would be a ruinous burden to employers.

Expanding Title IX Sports Regulations to Academics

In addition to introducing the Paycheck Fairness Act as a remedy for different average earnings, President Obama thinks that American women will do better in the workforce if they study math and science. And he has decided that the government should do something about it. The president wants to expand so-called gender parity under federal law beyond college athletics to courses in science, technology, engineering, and mathematics (STEM).

One of the president's first actions, in

The Paycheck Fairness Act, if enacted, would spawn a tidal wave of lawsuits and enmesh employers in endless litigation.

March 2009, was to set up a powerful White House Council on Women and Girls. It includes all cabinet secretaries as members and is headed by Assistant to the President and Senior Adviser Valerie Jarrett, and its mission is to "to enhance, support and coordinate the efforts of existing programs for women and girls."

A proposal to apply so-called Title IX gender equality to enrollment in math and science courses was discussed at a White House conference on June 23, 2010, the anniversary of Title IX, the 1972 amendment to the 1964 Civil Rights Act that was passed to ensure that women would not be discriminated against in any educational program or activity receiving federal funding.

In a White House statement entitled "Bringing Title IX to Classrooms and Labs," Jessie DeAro, senior policy analyst at the Office of Science and Technology Policy, wrote, "Title IX has been credited for dramatic increases in the participation of women and girls in athletics programs; however, Title IX also covers equity in educational programs.... Title IX was passed to ensure women and girls were not excluded from any educational program or activity receiving federal aid."

In 1979, the Department of Education interpreted Title IX to mean that all universities receiving federal funding must satisfy at least one requirement of a three-pronged test in order to be in compliance with the amendment.

This test, which has been applied so far only to intercollegiate athletic programs, requires that universities receiving federal funding do one of three things. They must either ensure that participation in intercollegiate athletic programs by gender is proportionate to undergraduate enrollment by gender; have a continuing tradition of expanding intercollegiate athletic programs for the underrepresented gender; or fully accommodate the athletic interests and abilities of the underrepresented gender.

Over the years, however, court rulings have placed strong emphasis on the proportionality requirement, and complying with this requirement has become the most effective way for universities to protect themselves against Title IX lawsuits. If 40 percent of the students are female, then 40 percent of the varsity sports slots have to go to women. In April 2010, the Department of Education ruled that colleges could not use surveys to show that women did not want to participate in sports.

As a result, Title IX has led universities around the country to eliminate a number of men's teams, thus taking away opportunities from male athletes. Title IX, as it is currently interpreted, fails to take into consideration the relative number of male and female students interested in participating in intercollegiate sports, as well as the relative athletic abilities of these students. Such measures would provide a much fairer standard for applying Title IX than proportionality.

The White House now is trying to work out how to apply existing gender-equity law on behalf of women beyond varsity sports to other areas. In a telephone conversation in summer 2009, Russlynn Ali, the Department of Education's assistant secretary for civil rights, told me that the move would require neither new legislation nor new regulations.

This looks like a solution – more government intervention in higher education – in search of a problem. While it is true that fewer undergraduate women than men major in STEM courses, there is no evidence that universities deny women equal opportunity to choose these fields of study – which, according to the Labor Department, can lead to lower average earnings than careers in law, finance, and medicine.

The White House does not appear to be concerned about whether men are deprived of taking literature, music, art, psychology, and biology by larger numbers of female majors. (They are not, just as women are not deprived of taking science classes by larger numbers of male majors.) If Title IX is going to be extended to academic subjects, why stop at math and science?

Many of the most admired and successful women in America – Secretaries of State Hillary Clinton and Condoleezza Rice, House Speaker Nancy Pelosi, eBay founder Meg Whitman – did not get degrees in STEM. Two world leaders, former British Prime Minister Margaret Thatcher and German Chancellor Angela Merkel, did get degrees in STEM, but they rose to power through a career in politics.

Stated differently, a STEM degree is not in itself a necessary step to success. Some college graduates with STEM degrees are today unemployed. If a STEM degree is neither necessary nor sufficient to progress in America, why is the government pushing this issue at all?

The answer is the uncontrollable urge of government to tell people what to do and how to run their lives. Washington knows better than ordinary Americans, or so we are told, and we ordinary Americans had better listen up.

The interagency task force led by the Department of Justice is examining expansion to STEM courses. Agencies participating include NASA, the Departments of Energy and Education, and the National Science Foundation.

NASA states on its Web site that it has not received any Title IX complaints, yet it has produced a manual, "Title IX and STEM: Promising Practices for Science, Technology, Engineering, and Mathematics," listing what it calls "best practices" for educational institutions, and it holds up these practices as examples to other universities.

NASA recommends that a Title IX coordinator be a member of a university's highest decision-making body and meet "weekly with the university president, provost, vice presidents, and deans." It is unlikely that it is a good use of university administrators' time to meet every week to discuss diversity.

And how many minutes must such meetings last, one may wonder, and how far into the minutiae of university administration shall the government intrude?

Quite far, NASA replies. It recommends in detail how a Title IX coordinator might go about her duties. She should be assisted by a full-time gender equity specialist to receive complaints. Staff from her office should be deployed to departments, labs, and centers of the university to observe "environments for morale and climate issues with both employees and students." One best practice is to fund departments based on the diversity of the student population.

The Title IX coordinator should also ensure the widespread availability of programs to prevent sexual harassment and violence against women, which feature prominently in the NASA manual. On page 26, the manual cites the example of one university's Oasis Program – note that the name of the program suggests a peaceful nourishing spot in what one assumes is a male-dominated, dry desert – which was set up to offer services to students and staff who are affected by "sexual assault, relationship violence, and stalking."

According to the manual, "The program's mission/goal is particularly effective in stating the need for its services, stating that the Oasis Program serves to 'contribute to the quality of the overall campus climate, to the safety, empowerment, and healing of victim/survivors, to the accountability of offenders, to the success of students remaining productive in their role as students and in the pursuit of their degrees, and to the success of staff and faculty remaining productive in their role as employees.'"

The NASA bureaucrats appear to believe that sexual harassment is a major reason that women do not major in STEM. The view is that men are aggressors, stalking and harassing women and rendering the classroom and laboratory an unpleasant place to work. That is supposedly why more women do not choose physics and chemistry.

Yet an examination of elite women's colleges, where the absence of men makes sexual harassment impossible, tells a different story.

At Bryn Mawr College, 4 percent of the 2010 graduating class chose to major in chemistry, 2 percent chose computer science, and 2 percent chose physics in recent years. At Smith College, half of one percent chose to major in physics, and 1.4 percent majored in computer science. At Barnard College, one-third of one percent majored in physics and astronomy in 2009 (data for 2010 were not available as of this writing), and 2 percent majored in chemistry.

Clearly, women have been able to enter and prosper in some previously male-dominated fields where sexual harassment did not appear to be an insuperable obstacle. Why, then, are women still "underrepresented" – if that is the right word – in some sciences, math, engineering, and technology?

Some women may avoid these fields because of their high math content. Boys have always scored higher than girls on math aptitude tests. In 1979, boys scored on average 43 points higher than girls on the SAT, declining to 35 points in the mid-1990s, a difference that persisted through 2009.

But there is a larger picture to behold. Women are doing well. Overall, their unemployment rate is more than two percentage points lower than men's. Women receive about 50 percent of medical and 45 percent of dentistry degrees, fields they have chosen to enter. In biology and biomedical sciences, they receive more degrees than men, namely 59 percent of BAs, 58 percent of MAs, and 51 percent of PhDs.

Moreover, in some cases, women are treated better than men when it comes to academic tenure decisions. Between 1999 and 2003, according to the National Academy of Sciences, although women represented only 11 percent of tenure-track job applicants in electrical engineering and 12 percent of applicants in physics, they received 32 percent and 20 percent of the job offers in these fields, respectively.

America COMPETES
Reauthorization Act of 2010

It is not only the administration that is trying to favor women in science. The America COMPETES Reauthorization Act of 2010, sponsored by Tennessee Democratic Rep. Bart Gordon, passed in the House of Representatives on May 28, 2010, and as of this writing is awaiting action in the Senate. The bill requires federal science agencies to record and publish information on the gender and race of recipients of university science grants.

Section 124 of the bill devotes nine pages to provisions on encouraging women to pursue education and careers in science and engineering. The section, titled "Fulfilling the Potential of Women in Academic Science and Engineering," establishes a workshop program intended to educate academics about the advantages of women majoring in science.

Here is how this would work. Program officers, members of grant review panels, institutions of higher education STEM department chairs, and other federally funded researchers would be invited to attend workshops – in Washington, D.C., or elsewhere –about minimizing the effects of gender in evaluating federal research grants and in the academic advancement of possible grant recipients.

The bill would require that "at least 1 workshop is supported every 2 years among the Federal science agencies in each of the major science and engineering disciplines supported by those agencies." All federal agencies that provide major research and development funding to universities would be required to comply.

Gordon wants the federal science agencies to invite the chairs of the science and engineering departments from at least the 50 colleges and universities receiving the most federal funding. Also invited would be members of federal research grant review panels, personnel managers from Department of Energy National Laboratories, and federal science agency program officers.

The workshops would focus on increasing participants' "awareness of the existence of gender bias in the grant-making process and the development of the academic record necessary to qualify as a grant recipient." The workshops also would encourage participants to work out ways to overcome these biases, such as mentoring female STEM students in undergraduate and graduate schools, as well as earlier in their education.

To make sure these science professors get the message, they would be required to complete surveys before and after attending the workshops and report any relevant policy changes that they have implemented at their universities.

The director of the White House Office of Science and Technology Policy would then send Congress a report evaluating the workshop program's effectiveness in reducing gender bias in federally funded research, including the results of the surveys and any policy changes made by the participants. The report would also report gender-related data trends for departments represented by any chair or employee who has participated in at least one workshop three or more years prior to the due date of the report. Finally, the report would include a list of STEM departments of higher education whose representatives attended the workshops held for their respective disciplines.

Naturally, the bill does not specifically declare that the information compiled in this report may be used in any way to influence the award of federal funds to institutions of higher education. But the bill's focus on collecting and reporting such detailed data on workshop attendance and demographic trends in science and engineering departments shows that the government finds this information highly relevant.

It is not at all implausible to speculate that

this data might at some point in the future be taken into consideration in making federal grant decisions. This puts pressure on universities to overlook the most qualified students in favor of those who will earn them the most grant money.

In fact, the bill devotes an entire section to data collection on federal research grants, by agency and by race and gender. The data would be published annually by the National Science Foundation. These provisions demonstrate some members' interest in the demographic trends related to the allocation of federal science funding.

Finally, the bill also requires that the direc-

Making female scientists beneficiaries of affirmative action devalues their credentials and ignores their true achievements.

tor of the Office of Science and Technology Policy develop a policy to "extend the period of grant support for federally funded researchers who have caregiving responsibilities" and provide them with "interim technical staff support" if they take a leave of absence.

Both expanding Title IX to academics and requiring busy university administrators to attend diversity workshops are attempts to artificially increase the numbers of women in science through federal regulation. But making female scientists beneficiaries of affirmative action devalues their credentials and ignores their true achievements.

If Congress and President Obama had their way, a PhD in STEM from a female scientist would be worth less than one from a male scientist. Weaker female scientists would be likely to get fewer articles published in peer-reviewed journals. Would they then be given the same positions and promoted through the ranks at the same rate as male scientists with more publications?

Both male and female students would suffer

from having less qualified professors, and America's competitiveness would diminish as talented men were deprived of jobs. The concept of parceling out jobs on the basis of gender and race makes a mockery of the idea that jobs are won through merit.

Discriminating against women, men, or minorities is already against the law. But absent demonstrated gender discrimination, it is absurd to try to artificially increase the number of female scientists through federal regulation, just as it would be absurd to try to channel more men into literature, communications, and women's studies.

American universities now give qualified students, regardless of gender and race, equal opportunities and encouragement to choose fields of study. Our university system is admired throughout the world, and foreigners flock to America to enroll. There is no better way to destroy our universities than by artificially ensuring gender parity in math and science.

*   *   *

Gender Quotas in the Financial Industry

First comes a push for quotas in science, then in employment. One of President Obama's signature pieces of legislation, the Dodd-Frank Wall Street Reform and Consumer Protection Act, could require race and gender employment ratios to be observed by private financial institutions that do business with the government. In a dramatic departure from current employment law, which forbids discrimination, "fair inclusion" of women and minorities, potentially leading to quotas, has been imposed on America's financial industry.

In addition to this law's well-publicized plans to establish more than a dozen new financial regulatory offices, Section 342 set up almost 30 Offices of Minority and Women Inclusion.

The departmental offices of the Treasury, the Federal Deposit Insurance Corporation, the Federal Housing Finance Agency, the 12 Federal Reserve regional banks, the Board of

Governors of the Federal Reserve System, the National Credit Union Administration, the Comptroller of the Currency, the Securities and Exchange Commission, the new Consumer Financial Protection Bureau – all got their own Office of Minority and Women Inclusion in the Dodd-Frank law.

What will be the mission of this new corps of federal monitors? The Dodd-Frank law sets it forth succinctly and simply – all too simply. The mission, it says, is to assure "to the maximum extent possible, the fair inclusion" of women and minorities, individually and through businesses they own, in the activities of the agencies, including contracting.

Each office will have its own director and staff, a senseless expansion of the bureaucracy, to develop policies promoting equal employment opportunities and racial, ethnic, and gender diversity of not just the agency's workforce, but also the workforces of its contractors and subcontractors. This means that not only would a financial institution have to prove its diversity, but the firms that shred its documents, clean its offices, and provide catering for office parties also would have to demonstrate "fair inclusion" of women and minorities.

How to define "fair" has bedeviled government administrators, university admissions officers, private employers, union shop stewards, and all other supervisors since time immemorial – or at least since Congress first undertook to prohibit discrimination in employment.

Title IX of the 1964 Civil Rights Act, as we saw in the prior section, defines fair as proportional to population. Financial institutions might have to meet a similar proportionality standard, regardless of the qualifications of applicants for jobs or contracts – or regardless of whether any women or minorities apply for the job.

Even if no women apply, "fair inclusion" is still the law of the land. The law's language recognizes this and tells agencies to search for underrepresented groups at women's colleges, job fairs in urban communities, girls' high schools, and through advertising in women's magazines.

Lest there be any narrow interpretation of Congress's intent, either by agencies or eventually by the courts, the law specifies that the "fair" employment test shall apply to "financial institutions, investment banking firms, mortgage banking firms, asset management firms, brokers, dealers, financial services entities, underwriters, accountants, investment consultants, and providers of legal services." That last appears to rope in law firms working for financial entities.

Contracts are defined expansively as "all contracts for all business and activities of an agency, at all levels, including contracts for the issuance or guarantee of any debt, equity, or security, the sale of assets, the management of the assets of the agency, the making of equity investments by the agency, and the implementation by the agency of programs to address economic recovery."

This latest attempt by Congress to dictate what "fair" employment means is likely to encourage administrators and managers, in government and in the private sector, to hire women and minorities for the sake of appearances, even if some new hires are less qualified than other applicants. The result is likely to be redundant hiring and a wasteful expansion of payroll overhead.

If the director decides that a contractor has not made a good-faith effort to include women and minorities in its workforce, he is required to contact the agency administrator and recommend that the contractor be terminated.

According to American Enterprise Institute resident fellow Christina Hoff Sommers, "This is going on everywhere. There are several bills pending in Congress such as Fulfilling the Potential of Women in Science and Engineering, the Paycheck Fairness Act, and now Section 342 of Dodd-Frank, that will empower a network of gender apparatchiks – but weaken critical national institutions."

Section 342's provisions are broad and vague, and they are certain to increase inefficiency in federal agencies. To comply, federal agencies are likely to find it easier to employ and contract with less qualified women and minorities, merely in order to avoid regulatory trouble. This would, in turn, decrease the agencies' efficiency, productivity, and output while increasing their costs.

Setting up these Offices of Minority and Women Inclusion is a troubling and unwarranted indictment of current law. By creating these new offices, Congress implied that existing law is insufficient. In fact, women and minorities already have an ample range of legal avenues to ensure that businesses engage in nondiscriminatory practices.

Cabinet-level departments already have individual Offices of Civil Rights and Diversity. In addition, the Equal Employment Opportunity Commission and the Labor Department's Office of Federal Contract Compliance are charged with enforcing racial and gender discrimination laws.

With the new financial regulation law, the federal government is moving from outlawing discrimination to setting up a system of quotas. Ultimately, the only way that financial firms doing business with the government would be able to comply with the law is by showing that a certain percentage of their workforce is female or minorities.

In a letter sent to Senate leaders about Section 342 of the Dodd-Frank law on July 13, 2010, four commissioners of the Equal Employment Opportunity Commission wrote, "The potential for abuse should be obvious, but sadly sometimes it is not to those who are unfamiliar with the workings of governmental and corporate bureaucracies. All too often, when bureaucrats are charged with the worthy task of preventing race or gender discrimination, they in fact do precisely the opposite: Consciously or unconsciously, they *require* discrimination by setting overly optimistic goals that can only be fulfilled by discriminating in favor of the groups the goals are supposed to benefit."

The commissioners continue, "In this case, the bureaucrats are not even being asked to prevent discrimination, but to ensure 'fair inclusion.' The likelihood that it will in fact promote discrimination is overwhelming."

The new Offices of Minority and Women Inclusion represent a major change in employment law by imposing gender and racial quotas on the financial industry.

Gender Quotas in Health Care Law

Visit any retirement home in America, and you will be struck by a self-evident fact: The vast majority of residents are women. Ask them what they would like to see, and chances are you will hear the obvious response: "More men."

The federal government is not listening to these women. Or to men, for that matter. Men do not come close to living as long as women. The vast majority of retirement-age Americans are women. On average, men's life expectancy is five years shorter than women's. When young, men are more likely to be killed in homicides or in military service. Men are more likely than women to die from unintentional injuries or suicide and have a higher binge-drinking rate. Later in life, men, like women, suffer from heart attacks and various forms of cancer. Some forms of cancer, such as prostate cancer, are unique to men.

Uncle Sam may be looking for a few good men, but Uncle Sam does not want to keep them alive very long. Uncle Sam is partial to women and wants to keep them alive much longer. The Patient Protection and Affordable Care Act, signed into law by President Obama in March 2010, mentions seven offices and

---

A woman who chooses a part-time job with a flexible schedule in order to have time both for her family and her career thinks of herself as successful. But to feminists, she is a failure.

---

coordinating committees especially for women – and not one for men. The word "breast" is mentioned 42 times in the act, and the word "prostate" does not even warrant one. The new law does not address men's health and the unique health challenges faced by American men today.

The new law creates full employment for professionals specializing in – you guessed it – women's health. Within the Department of Health and Human Services, the law refers to three Offices of Women's Health; one Coordinating Committee on Women's Health, with senior representatives from each of the department's agencies and offices; and one National Women's Health Information Center, to facilitate information exchange as well as "coordinate efforts to promote women's health programs and policies with the private sector."

Plus, the Food and Drug Administration has its own Office of Women's Health, as does the Centers for Disease Control and Prevention (CDC). These seven offices are supposed to promote women's health and identify women's health projects that deserve federal funding.

If federal bureaucracies and spending can extend life expectancies, American women will live forever. The budgets in the new offices created by the new law appear to be unlimited – the statute simply says that "there are authorized to be appropriated *such sums as may be necessary* (italics added) for each of the fiscal years 2010 through 2014."

Not only is the government overtly favoring women's health over men's, but provisions in the reform law ensure that the government will be able to provide incentives for the private sector to do the same through the National Women's Health Information Center and the Offices on Women's Health. The secretary will also be empowered to enter into contracts with and make grants to "public and private entities, agencies, and organizations" in order to enable the Office on Women's Health to carry out its activities. Money talks, and these provisions will encourage researchers and hospitals to neglect men's health in favor of women's in order to contract with and receive grants from the federal government.

The other two women's health offices within the Department of Health and Human Services are located at the National Institutes of Health (NIH) and the Office of the Administrator of the Health Resources and Services Administration (HRSA). These offices will monitor NIH and HRSA activity relating to women's health and identify women's health projects that the NIH or the HRSA might support. The NIH office also will consult with "health professionals, nongovernmental organizations, consumer organizations, women's health professionals, and other individuals and groups" to develop women's health policy, while the HRSA office will coordinate activities relating to "health care provider training, health service delivery, research, and demonstration projects" for women's health issues.

The Offices of Women's Health within the CDC and the FDA will monitor and promote all CDC and FDA activities relating to women's health, and their directors will serve on the Department of Health and Human Services Coordinating Committee on Women's Health.

Many people, including the female residents of retirement homes, might ask: Who in their right mind would set up countless government bureaucracies and spend untold billions of dollars to help women, but not men, live longer?

The answer, sadly, is that the authors of the new health care law may not be out of their minds, but they are out of touch with America. The authors of the new law find fault with all that is America, and they seek to deconstruct America and rebuild it in their own worldviews. In that distorted world, men are evil and not to be aided; women, in contrast, are perpetual victims and in perpetual need of government assistance.

Both men and women want everyone to live longer. But the new health care law was written for a world where the government seemingly plans to give more money for women's health problems than for men's. And

American taxpayers, both male and female, are going to pay billions of dollars for that world filled with powerful bureaucracies teeming with health care professionals preoccupied with women's health care.

CONCLUSION

Americans live in two worlds. One is the everyday world in which they work, study, play, laugh, cry, love, and hate. In that world, women are more likely than men to succeed. Women, on average, do better in school, better in work, better in life. Women triumph in everyday America.

The other America is the distortion constructed by radical feminists and Washington politicians. These politicians make a career out of telling women that they are defeated. No Washington government official bothers to hail the victory of women in everyday America. Instead, they revel in lies and distortions. They tell America that women need government help. They tell America that Washington has the answer: more laws and more regulations designed to give women additional advantages at the expense of men.

The second America, the distorted America, would not matter if the federal government were unimportant in our economy and our society. But Washington makes sure that it is important. It makes sure that all aspects of everyday America – the America in which women are triumphant – are put under the thumb of some Washington bureaucrat.

The message of women as victims contradicts the view of women held by the original feminists who fought for the right to vote, the right to work while pregnant and with small children, and the right to equal wages. Fifty years ago, it was permitted to advertise jobs with one salary for men and another for women. Times have changed, and now that is not only illegal, but it is culturally unacceptable.

But the viewpoint of employers who thought that women were worth less than men lives on among current feminists, who imply that women can only succeed with government assistance – in math and science, in financial industry employment, in health care. Anti-discrimination laws are not sufficient, they say, and they call for quotas. A woman's choice of less time at the office and more time at home with family is not considered an opportunity but a societal problem calling for a government solution.

American women, so we are told, cannot succeed on our own. We need the protection of the federal government in every aspect of our lives.

Women face conflicting realities in America. On the one hand, we succeed in our daily lives. On the other hand, we have our federal government belittling us, telling us that we are defeated, that we are victims, that our efforts are hopeless, that we cannot succeed.

Simply stated, the federal government wants to steal our earned success and ascribe it to official intervention. It wants to brand us as losers in search of help, with the federal government being the brave knight to rescue the American damsel in distress. American women, so we are told, cannot succeed on our own. We need the protection of the federal government in every aspect of our lives. And, like little girls, we had better listen and do as we are told.

It is time for American women to stand up. Government programs that attempt to guarantee outcomes favorable to women undermine the achievements and choices that we make every day without such programs. They do not help us; they harm us. Like all Americans, we succeed in our daily lives not because the federal government guarantees our success, but precisely because it does not.

First American edition published in 2010 by Encounter Books,
an activity of Encounter for Culture and Education, Inc.,
a nonprofit, tax exempt corporation.
Encounter Books website address: www.encounterbooks.com

Manufactured in the United States and printed on
acid-free paper. The paper used in this publication meets
the minimum requirements of ANSI/NISO Z39.48–1992
(R 1997) (*Permanence of Paper*).

FIRST AMERICAN EDITION

LIBRARY OF CONGRESS CATALOGING-IN-PUBLICATION DATA

Furchtgott-Roth, Diana.
How Obama's gender policies undermine America / by Diana
Furchtgott-Roth.
p.   cm.
ISBN-13: 978-1-59403-539-5 (pbk. : alk. paper)
ISBN-10: 1-59403-539-3 (pbk. : alk. paper)
1. Women—Government policy—United States. 2. Sex discrimination
against men—United States. 3. Women—United States—Economic
conditions—21st century. 4. Feminism—United States—History—
21st century. 5. Equality—United States—History—21st century.
I. Title.
HQ1236.5.U6F87 2010
305.32—dc22
2010031021

10 9 8 7 6 5 4 3 2 1